This Is The Day!

This Is The Day!

Sermons for Lent and Easter
based on the Second Lessons
for Cycle A

Kimberly van Driel

CSS Publishing Company
Lima, Ohio

THIS IS THE DAY

FIRST EDITION
Copyright © 2025 by
CSS Publishing Company, Inc.

Library of Congress Cataloging-in-Publication Data
Names: Miller van Driel, Kimberly, 1978- author
Title: This is the day! : sermons for Lent and Easter based on the second
  lessons for Cycle A / Kimberly van Driel.
Description: First edition. | Lima, Ohio : CSS Publishing Company, [2025]
Identifiers: LCCN 2025029410 (print) | LCCN 2025029411 (ebook) | ISBN
  9780788031335 paperback | ISBN 9780788031342 adobe pdf
Subjects: LCSH: Bible. New Testament--Sermons | Common lectionary (1992).
  Year C | Lent--Sermons | Easter--Sermons
Classification: LCC BS2341.55 .M54 2025 (print) | LCC BS2341.55 (ebook)
LC record available at https://lccn.loc.gov/2025029410
LC ebook record available at https://lccn.loc.gov/2025029411

For more information about CSS Publishing Company resources, visit our website at www.csspub.com, email us at csr@csspub.com, or call (800) 241-4056.

e-book:
ISBN-13: 978-0-7880-3134-2
ISBN-10: 0-7880-3134-1

ISBN-13: 978-0-7880-3133-5
ISBN-10: 0-7880-3133-3   PRINTED IN USA

With gratitude to God for my grandparents,
Mary Ann Franzen
Lavern Franzen +
Robert and Alice Miller +

Table Of Contents

Preface

It is a courageous preacher that would choose the second readings for the Lent and Easter cycle of the Revised Common Lectionary in Year A. In the lectionary's design, the assigned epistle texts complement vivid stories from the Old Testament as well as the gospels and dive into deep theological waters. Sin and grace, death and life, suffering and glory, sacrifice and salvation, election and obedience — all of these themes await the preacher who digs into these passages from Scripture. So do the exegetical challenges of interpreting a passage selected out of its literary context and placed within a liturgical one. Some of the readings for this season — I think particularly of the selections from Romans 4 and 5 in the early Sundays of Lent — have deeply contested interpretations among the scholars who know the most about these texts. Conscientious preachers will ignore none of these difficulties!

Still, for those who wish to dig into them, these readings have much to say about what it means to live with the death and resurrection of Jesus Christ as an ever-present reality.

In this collection of sermons, I have tried to allow this reality to shine. These sermons emerge from my own experience as a Lutheran pastor in majority white, working-class to middle-class settings and not all of the stories, examples, or applications will speak in every other context. (I should also note that in the stories that I tell of my own experience, names and many significant details have been changed!) Still, I do think that it is part of the universal human condition to settle for less than the grace of God in Jesus Christ and it is the unending desire of God to intrude on us with more — more grace, more hope, more courage. I hope that the sermons that follow inspire readers to think about these dynamics in their own context.

Preaching is never the work of a single person but is the communal work of the church. I want to thank my siblings in Christ that helped this project come to fruition. My husband, Edwin van Driel, encouraged me daily as this project was ongoing. The Thursday morning Bible study at First English Lutheran Church in Butler, Pennsylvania, tackled 1 Peter (assigned for the Easter seasons) during the summer of 2024. Their vigorous conversation and questions inspired some of the sermons offered here. David Runk, president/editor at CSS, helped keep me on track. I thank them all for their encouragement and support.

This Is The Day!

"Salvation. Don't be caught dead without it."

So proclaimed the digital billboard along the road I take to church every day. Skillfully placed at an intersection where traffic would often need to pause to take notice, the sign's message was accompanied by the picture of a cross. Over the course of a few seconds, the image would dissolve and the picture of an airplane would appear, each arm of the cross becoming the wing and the head of the cross the cockpit. Since for some months I saw this billboard at least twice a day, I've had some opportunity to think about its message. It suggests that salvation is something that we can possess, that it is something like a ticket voucher, good for travel after we die, away from here to what is above, to heaven, where we can be with God forever. The cross speaks of what Jesus has done in the past; the airplane speaks to the undepictable future; the present, meanwhile, is the place where we accept Jesus' death for our sins in exchange for heaven. Many of us have been taught that that is what "salvation" in Christ means; it means going to heaven when we die as opposed to "the other place," which, according to that billboard's current image programming ("Do you know where your soul is going?") looks like a massive bonfire.

Many of us were taught to think of salvation in just these terms, and it is true that the good news of God has something to say about life, death, and life after death. On Ash Wednesday, we confront our mortal reality, remembering that we are dust, and to dust we shall return. But this Lent, this Ash Wednesday, I believe that the word of God has something more to say about salvation than as a promised future in heaven. Our Second Lesson from Second Corinthians declares "Now is the acceptable time! Now is the day of salvation!" This Lent, God invites us to see, to receive, salvation today. In the present. Now. Today is the day that God is making us whole, making us new, because even today Jesus is reaching out to us to reconcile us to God, to put away our sin and guilt so that we can live at peace with God and with one another. So, salvation is not something that we file away for later but is a gift of God for the present moment. We get to live with that gift each and every day, but the season of Lent invites us to be more conscious of it.

There are, however, several challenges in doing that. For one, "now" does not often feel very heavenly — quite the opposite, in fact! Today, we may open the news app to read about the most recent school shooting or threats of violence. Today, we may hear of more rumblings of war in places on the earth that have already suffered too much. Today, families who don't have enough food may be just as hungry as they were yesterday. Today may be the day that we fell off the wagon, where we got up and lost our temper with our spouse or our children. Today, for someone in our community, salvation may look like a bottle of Narcan before it looks like anything else.

Don't be caught dead without salvation, warned the sign. The reality is that that there are many ways to be caught by the powers of death, by those things that tear away at God's good creation, and only some of them involve the end of respiration. Saint Paul, who wrote second Corinthians, named a few: afflictions, hardships, calamities, beatings, imprisonments, riots, labors, sleepless nights, hunger, dishonor, ill repute, and being treated as an unknown, dying, punished, sorrowful, poor imposter." Earlier in his letter to Corinth — before we get to this somewhat confusing passage that the church always reads on Ash Wednesday — he wrote that he was so sick and tired of the whole thing that he was ready to quit and despaired even of life itself. So how was it that he could say that "now" was the day of salvation? That now was an "acceptable time?" What is "acceptable" to God about hardships and calamity?

This is the acceptable time, the day of salvation, because this is the day that God in Christ reaches into this world and out to us who are caught in the powers of death. This is the acceptable time because the one who knew no sin walked in solidarity with sinful people and even died a sinner's death. God in Christ is making this the acceptable day because God in Christ reaches out to us. The cross does not prefigure an airplane, set to deliver us from the earth and all its troubles. The cross is the revelation of God's love for us in the midst of trouble, the sign that nothing will separate us from grace.

Saint Paul knew this, deep in his bones. He'd been saved by Jesus Christ, once for all on the cross — but that saving power showed up in his own life more than just once. He'd been a persecutor of the church, a man of violence — until the day the risen Jesus showed up in his path, struck him blind, and then revealed a new commission to him as a preacher to the church he once tried to destroy — and new opportunities for the hardships that it seems he loves to name. But those moments of despair became for him new moments to discover what it means to be saved now, to have life not in our own hands but safe in the hands of a God who raises the dead who calls into existence the things that do not exist. And so, right alongside all the trials, Paul would also experience purity, knowledge, patience, kindness, holiness of spirit, genuine love, truthful speech, the power of God, using the weapons of righteousness in both hands for the sake of being who he really was, a well-known, living, rejoicing, person who possessed everything worth having and who was willing to give it away.

In our church, every Ash Wednesday, we offer the "imposition of ashes," marking foreheads with the sign of the cross. In the brief time that we wear them — the ash doesn't last all that long — we are like walking billboards. The ash advertises our mortality. It tells of lives that are far from perfect, of a "now" that is broken. As is the reminder that we are always being "caught dead" and that someday, we will die. But it's not just ash that we wear. It's ash in the shape of a cross, the sign of shameful death that God made into the means of life.

This year, when I receive these ashes, when I impose them, I imagine them dissolving like a digital image on my forehead and on all who receive, dissolving into the picture of those places in our lives where we might imagine God cannot possibly be. Christ with us in our addiction. Christ with us in our shame. Christ with us in our despair and our guilt. Christ with us in those bitter moments where we have failed our families, our friends, our callings. He made him to be sin who knew no sin, Paul declared. Christ didn't have to be here with us in these places, but this is where he chooses to be. And this is salvation: we will never be caught in the powers of death without being caught by the promise of Jesus.

Now is the acceptable time. He makes it so.

Now is the day.

Amen.

Family Ties: Adam And Christ

I once attended the installation of a faculty member to a prestigious administrative position at a theological school. The candidate was relatively young but possessed for his age a resume rich with educational degrees, church service, and administrative experience. He was moving up from another school with accolades and blessings from former students and colleagues. At the ceremony, speeches from the search committee, the school's board of directors, and local pastors testified to his intelligence and leadership skills. I don't know if you have ever had the experience of learning that you were in the presence of someone who is uniquely excellent at what they do, but that's how it seemed to me at that moment. I was watching someone *great* be installed into this role. So great, in fact, that I couldn't help but make the comparisons between my talents and his, my accomplishments and his — comparisons by which I found myself wanting.

Then the good professor's wife shared a few words.

"You have heard all of these great things about my husband," I remember her saying, "But what you need to know is that he is also a forgiven sinner who is loved by Jesus Christ."

With that, the entire room exhaled a breath of appreciative "Amen," by which we meant, "Yes, that's me, too."

Because somehow, with those few words, she pointed us to a truth about who we are in relationship to God, which is to say, the fundamental truth about what it means to be human, period. God has made us good, but we have fallen short of all that God has made us to be: we are sinners. God has not, however, allowed sin to be the final word. God has redeemed us by sending Jesus to heal and forgive so that we can be *forgiven* sinners, so that we can be part of a whole new humanity that goes by the name of "Jesus Christ."

This is most certainly true, whether the list of our accomplishments is long or short, or whether we are young or old. It is true whatever our ethnicity. It is even true whether we have a long rap sheet or could pass a criminal background check with flying colors. It is true whatever our family arrangements.

Why? Because we are all a part of the human family — or, you might say, *Adam's* family. Today our reading from Romans reminds us that it is through "one man" that the power of sin and death came into the world. Saint Paul, who wrote Romans, is thinking here of the first man, whose temptation we hear about in the first reading from Genesis. Many of you will remember that story: how God created the first humans and put them in a marvelous garden, where they could eat of any tree except the tree of the knowledge of good and evil, and how the serpent tempted the first couple in the garden to eat of the tree. For much of the Christian tradition — and clearly this was true of Saint Paul as well — this story helps explain how it was that sin, evil, and death came to be part of God's good creation. Now, Romans doesn't explain *how* it is that sin and death came to affect everyone. The point is that it affects *everyone.* Everyone, whether Jew or Gentile. Everyone, including those who lived *before* God gave the law, the commandments that helped us know what sin is. Everyone, who lived after the giving of the law but never had an opportunity to hear or learn. Sin is not about what you know or don't know. It's a part of being human. We are all part of Adam's family, under the powers of sin and death.

Sometimes the news that we are all sinners comes as a relief — as it did when I was sitting in the faculty installation. From a human perspective, we have different resumes, different successes, different contributions, some which seem good, some which seem less so. From God's perspective, we all share the same human condition of Adam and are all in need.

But at other times, this news that we are all part of Adam's family is unnerving. If we are all part of the same family, then from God's perspective, none of us are better than the other. From God's perspective, I am not better than those who reside at the county jail four blocks down. My culture is not better than other cultures. My resume is not better than others' achievements. God will not allow us, as members of Adam's family, to compare ourselves to one another to the result of despair or pride.

What God *will* allow instead is for us to take comfort and refuge in being part of another family, a new human family, Jesus' family. Jesus was born into the world as part of Adam's family. As the gospel from Matthew reminds us today, he too was subject to the temptation that Adam experienced and that all of us experience: the temptation not to live within the limits that God places for us, the temptation to want to be our own gods. But where Adam and all others — including ourselves — give in to the power of sin, Jesus was faithful to his calling to live as God's child. He refused to relinquish his identity as the beloved Son of God, even when it led him to the cross. On that cross, he became subject to the powers of death that human sin brought into the world. He suffered condemnation though he did not earn or deserve it. But God raised him up. By God's power, Jesus' faithfulness, his obedience, his death, and his life have become a gift for us, a gift that is more powerful than the power of sin that came through Adam. That is grace, the gift of life. That is the gift of a relationship with God that endures through human brokenness. By one man came death to all, but God, who has a sense of symmetry and symbol, sent another man — the one who was both divine and human. Through this one comes life to all.

In the Lutheran tradition from which I hail, we have a saying that encapsulates the reality of being part of both Adam's family and Christ's family. We are, we love to say, both sinners and saints. We are sinners who fall short, but we are saints who have been also brought into the right relationship with

God. At any given moment on this side of glory, both tendencies are at work in us — both sin and grace. Sometimes you will see more of one than the other, though. The volunteer who constantly works at the soup kitchen may seem like a saint to her fellow volunteers. She is! But when she heads home to her family and loses her temper, she might seem more the sinner. She is! The Old Lutheran store, which specializes in selling Lutheran merch, sells a temporary tattoo sticker that from one side reads "sinner." Turn your perspective 180° and it reads "saint." We are both!

We are both saints and sinners. In Lent, we acknowledge our sin, but even more, we celebrate its overcoming in Jesus' death and resurrection. Romans wants us to know that sin is big, but grace is bigger.

"What you need to know is that he is a forgiven sinner, loved by Jesus Christ," said the good professor's spouse. With the name of Jesus Christ, she named something far better than even his impressive accomplishments; she named the source of life and love, which can never be earned but can only be received as a gift. We were born part of Adam's family. The abundance of God's grace makes us part of Jesus' family.

Those folks who seem like they are living such better lives than you are; whose credentials are more impressive, or who seem to have a greater share of the spotlight – are they different from us? What you need to know about them is that they are forgiven sinners in need of Jesus Christ, just like you. For them Christ lived. For them Christ died.

Those folks who seem like they aren't living well, whose habits annoy you, whose choices offend you, or whose crimes were reported yesterday – what about them? What you need to know is that they are forgiven sinners, whom Christ loves and for whom Christ died.

And you? You are a forgiven sinner, whom Christ loves and for whom Christ died. You are part of his family.

Amen.

Lent 2
Romans 4:1-5; 13-17

Family Ties: Not By Birth But Gracious Belonging

"I've been a member here for ten years, but sometimes it feels as though I'll always be a newcomer, because I wasn't born and raised here," said Latoya to the rest of the room. The members of First Lutheran Church's council were gathered with the new interim pastor, and they were making introductions: name, length of time as a member, ways involved in the congregation, reasons for joining or staying. At 42, Latoya was the youngest one in the room, and in another context, Latoya's words might have sounded harsh or blaming, but Clive and Mitchell had just introduced themselves before it was Latoya's turn and their stories set hers in context — and set off laughter around the circle. Clive had been baptized in the congregation as a baby 75 years before; his great-grandfather had donated a parcel of land for the first parsonage. Mitchell admittedly "was born a Presbyterian" but his family had joined First Lutheran when they moved to the community when Mitch was three. In fact, one of his earliest memories was of the old bathroom in the sacristy that had a chain you had to pull from the ceiling in order to flush the toilet. Now in his eighties, Mitch was the only one in the room who could remember it.

"How much do you think being a lifetime member of this congregation matters — to a sense of belonging, for who gets to make decisions?" asked interim Pastor Paula after introductions were done. They wanted — as most congregations wanted to be — a congregation for everyone. That said, though, Latoya *did* have a point about still feeling new after ten years. "Think about that quilt," said Brenda, who had been part of the congregation for twenty years, speaking of a fading wall hanging on the stairwell to the basement. It had been made for the congregation's hundredth anniversary, and each quilt block contained the embroidered name of someone who was a member at that time. Some people in the congregation knew exactly where they could find the names of their parents or grandparents in the blue thread. "That quilt, that history, occupies a lot of precious wall space. Sometimes it feels like a symbol of who really belongs."

The council was quiet for a while, uncomfortable.

Then Shirley, who grew up in the congregation, spoke up.

"My mama's name is on that quilt," she said quietly, "So I guess I'm one of those old timers. How my mama's name is there is the story I want to tell. My mama came here with her mama. Her mama was divorced at a time when being divorced usually marked you as a bad woman. Grandma never got used to the whispers and stares in town. She hated to go anywhere, but she wanted mama and my uncle to know God and so one day she brought us to this church. The people here? They didn't stare. They didn't whisper. They welcomed mama to Sunday school like all the other kids, and that is why my family stayed, because we felt like this was God's family. So, yes, I can find my mama's name on that quilt, but I belong because of Jesus, and I hope that when we think about who belongs, that that is what will matter.

II.

First Lutheran wasn't the first congregation to wrestle with questions of belonging. Who stays? What makes you a part of things? A church planter, Pastor Paul, faced with all the churches he founded, and the first Christian church of Rome was no different.

Gathered together as a church were people with a Jewish background and people with a Gentile background. Together, they worshiped the same God, but there were always questions about what it meant to belong. In this case, the question was not just about who had influence in the local congregation.

Belonging in this case was about belonging to *God*, being right with God, being part of God's family. All of them — Jews and Gentiles — believed in the crucified and risen Jesus. But there were some important differences between the two groups. The Jewish members of the community could find the names of their ancestors in the genealogies of the Old Testament. You know some of the chapters in the Old Testament that read "so and so begat, so and so begat?" We often skip those chapters when we read, but some members of the Roman church knew *exactly* where to go in scripture to find their ancestors' names.

The names of the Gentiles would never be included in the genealogies of course. So, there were some who said that while there was nothing you could do about that, there were nevertheless ways to make the Gentiles part of the same family. The Gentiles could be required to keep to the law, the Torah, that had been given by God and passed through the family, circumcising the males, keeping kosher food laws, observing special holidays and festivals. Jesus, himself a Jew, had done such things.

Knowing how powerful such ideas were, Pastor Paul wrote a letter to proclaim the gospel. The good news of God is that we are made part of God's family because of Jesus Christ. Trust in Jesus is what matters. Faith makes a Christian, not a work of the law.

In fact, Pastor Paul noted, it had always been this way. In the part of the book of Romans we heard today, Paul pointed to the *original* ancestor: Abraham. God promised a family to Abraham, not because Abraham had done anything in particular, not because he was circumcised, not because he only ate certain kinds of foods. God promised a family to Abraham because…God promised a family to Abraham. God's promise, however, seemed anything but straightforward. Abraham was old. His wife was barren. At 75 years old and 99 years old, they had no children.

But Abraham believed God. This, God counted as the relationship. This, Genesis says, Romans says, "God reckoned as righteousness."

It's trust in God, said Pastor Paul, that makes a family of faith, and everyone in faith has an ancestor in Abraham.

III.

I do not know what belonging in your congregation looks like, or what issues your community struggles with, but it has been my experience that wherever Christians gather, questions of belonging and identity inevitably rise. "I'll really belong to my church when I am married and have children," I've heard some people say. Sometimes belonging is a matter of worship style, or a matter of ethnicity, or a certain kind of literacy in reading and singing hymns. Sometimes belonging is about theology or signing up for particular creeds or confessions. Often, who belongs is a matter of struggle and pain.

That's why, this Lent, it comes as such good news to be reminded by Pastor Paul that God makes us part of the family by grace. By grace God chose Abraham. By grace God sent Jesus to save Jews and Gentiles, Shirley's divorced grandmother and Clive's long faithful family. By grace, God sends Jesus to you and to me. Freely, God sent Jesus Christ into this world. Freely, Christ stretched his arms upon the cross. Freely, God made Jesus' tomb the ground of a new creation. Nothing compelled God to do any of this. God does it for us in freedom. Receiving his promise, trusting his choice, we belong.

This is the second Sunday of Lent, so we are well into the Lenten season. I imagine, however, that there may be some of you who are looking for a Lenten discipline, something to do to mark the season. Sometimes, people like to "give things up" for Lent. At its worst, "giving things up" can be a rote ritual. At its best, it's a practice that helps us be more conscious of who God is and how we are connected to God.

So, today, let me suggest this: search your hearts, and ask yourselves whether there are standards of belonging in your congregation that are something other than the grace-filled promise of life in Christ. Consider giving them up for Lent.

Revel instead in this good news: faith makes us part of the family.

Amen.

He Died For
Us Weak Ones

The junior firefighter had completed multiple courses at the local fire academy and regularly went to weekly training at his local volunteer department. He loved the technical aspects of the work: how to put on gear, how to assess danger, how to communicate with other responders. He liked the thought of being a hero. Since he was only sixteen years old, he did not think too much about the risks — physical and psychological — that come with a first responder.

Then came the day when the department was called to a bad structure fire. Since he was a minor, state law prevented him from entering the house, but it was his first opportunity to watch seasoned officers assess the risk to themselves in crafting their response. Thankfully, there were no people or animals in the burning house that needed to be rescued, but the whole situation got the young firefighter thinking. What would it be like to risk your life for someone else? What if that someone else was, for example, a mass murderer — would he risk his life then? That seemed like a ridiculous waste. Then he considered how he would feel if the trapped person had knowledge that could cure cancer. Would there be any situation so dangerous where he would *not* try to save that person, knowing that that person could save many more lives? What if the person was an innocent child? How could he ever stay on the sidelines then?

Such wonderings and questions are common among those who put themselves in harm's way. For others, they may have been the substance of an assignment for philosophy class. For today, however, I want to use those wonderings as a window into the deep grace of God. Our reading for Romans tells us that indeed a life has been given for us. Christ has died for us, stretching out his arms upon the cross. He has done this so that our relationship with God might be healed and so that we might be saved from the hopelessness of a life apart from God.

What's more, Jesus gives his life for us "while we were still sinners." That is to say, while we were still people who did not have anything to make us worth saving. We did not have skills to add to God's glory that would make us worth saving. We were, Romans says, "weak," not even knowing what we didn't know, not even aware of how broken our relationship with God really was. We were "ungodly." Ungodly people do not recognize the love of God; they do not worship God; they are incapable of giving thanks to God. We were, Romans says, God's "enemies;" our relationship to God was not only a matter of indifference but outright opposition.

On a human level, grace this deep is offensive to our sensibilities. The ponderings of the young firefighter can help us see this offense, I think. We tend to evaluate lives according to their innocence or guilt, according to their usefulness or their worth. Paul, who wrote Romans, knew those kinds of evaluations. It was utterly crazy to think that anyone would easily give up their lives. Rarely would someone die for a righteous person. Sometimes, such an exchange might be dared for a good person. What Paul doesn't need to say is that it is utterly unimaginable that anyone would give their life to save an enemy that hated them. If God worked the way that we do, the love of God would be given to those who are loving. The favor of God would be given to those who are grateful. The joy of God's presence would be given to those who are holy.

God's grace, however, does not work that way. As Martin Luther said in his *Heidelberg Disputation*, "The love of God does not find, but creates, that which is pleasing to it…the love of God which lives in man loves sinners, evil persons, fools, and weaklings in in order to make them righteous, good, wise, and strong. Rather than seeking its own good, the love of God flows forth and bestows good. Therefore, sinners are attractive because they are loved, they are not loved because they are attractive."[1] Or, as a well-loved spiritual put it, "When I was sinking down, sinking down, sinking down, Christ laid aside his crown for my soul." This is what the love of the cross is. During Lent, we get an opportunity to become more conscious of that love, more aware of how different God's love is that human logic, than human reasoning. *While we were still sinners, Christ gave up his life for us.*

There are many things, no doubt, that are amazing about this kind of grace, but for the rest of our time today, I want to think about two things in particular, two ways in which this is good news for all of us.

First, because Christ's love is for sinners, we never have to worry that there are people who might be beyond his reach. We never have to worry that we might fall to a place where we are beyond his reach! I often hear these concerns from folks who look on the siblings, friends, children, or cousins that they consider "wayward," folks that they fear somehow might miss out on salvation. Sometimes I hear it as folks reflect on the guilt of their own past misdeeds. Romans is telling us today that our waywardness has never been an obstacle for God's redeeming work. God goes *to* the lost. God sends Christ to rescue even those who seem to oppose him. There's an old saying about never putting a period where God is putting a comma. God's grace simply doesn't have the kinds of limits that our grace does. That's one facet of this good news.

The second good news is that when God comes in Christ to rescue us, God comes truly to free us from sin. God does not come in Christ to redeem us so that we can spend time thinking about how worthless we really are in God's sight. Rather, God in Christ comes so that we can truly receive his goodness, wisdom, and strength. I think this is why Romans tells us that we can boast in our sufferings — knowing that suffering pro-

1   Martin Luther, "Heidelberg Disputation," in *Luther's Works, Vol. 31, Career of the Reformer 1*, Philadelphia: Fortress, 1957, 57.

duces endurance, and then character, and then hope. Because God is making all things right in the relationship, we do not have to worry that suffering is a sign of God's displeasure or anger. We do not have to receive suffering as a kind of corrective to bring us back into line. Sufferings are not sent as a trial to purify us from sin or to remind us of our weakness. Rather, sufferings can be — despite all evidence to the contrary — simply received as yet another place where God is turning the world upside down with love.

It's for sinners that Christ gives all. It's in the midst of suffering that God does God's best work. It's not logical to our minds, but then again, grace never is. Thanks be to God, grace is never logical but is abundant.

Amen.

Wake Up And Live

At the age of 88, my great uncle Tom received bad news: his liver had stopped making a critical enzyme that we need to live. Without it, he could expect a slow decline and finally, death.

Receiving this news coincided with the sale of his house and his plan to move into an apartment in the same retirement community where his sister, my grandmother, lived. There was no changing the arrangement. The papers were signed. His possessions were in boxes. The moving truck was arranged. An eminently practical person, he moved into his new apartment and unpacked nothing other than what he would need for his last few weeks of life. He enrolled himself in hospice and did not bother to introduce himself to his neighbors, who called him the dead man in apartment 422.

Death, however, did not happen as planned. His liver apparently started making the needed enzyme again. He began to feel better. He unpacked his belongings and set up his apartment. And since he was going to live, he decided he better get to know his neighbors. He ordered food from the facility's kitchen, sent my grandma out for a couple of bottles of gin, and invited all of his neighbors to a party to celebrate the life of the living man in apartment 422.

This is not a resurrection story, because Uncle Tom's reprieve, was, of course, temporary. He lived thirteen more years until the age of 101. But the dramatic change in his circumstances, the celebration of life, the move from closed-in, boxed up, has always been a parable for me of the decisive change Jesus brings to our lives. That the dynamics of death and resurrection will happen for us fully in the future, but God gives us something of their decisive change *now* in the midst of his life.

Our Ephesians text today describes this in terms of darkness and light, sleeping and being awake, death and life. "Once you were darkness, but now, in the Lord, you are light. Live as children of the light." And "Awake, O sleeper, rise from death, and Christ will give you light." In the twenty-first-century, we have a hard time imagining what these words mean; we have so much artificial light that in many places we can hardly see the stars. But in the ancient world the nighttime meant complete absence of sight. The darkness meant the ability to hide: to hide from one's neighbors. To hide one's choices. Without the freedom to move, one could close in on the self. And so became a metaphor for a self that was closed in on itself, unwilling to see its impact, unwilling to connect with others. Disobedient: unwilling to listen.

Once we were all like this, Ephesians is telling us. We were all like the almost dead man in apartment 422. I think of so many congregations, making their way these days under the diagnosis of church decline: shrinking budgets, decaying buildings, fear of their (sometimes new, sometimes very different) neighbors. I think of the ways those congregations can sometimes collapse upon themselves in infighting and inward focus, so that the people of their neighborhood have no idea who they are or why they are there or the God they serve.

I think of those who take, as a measure of their own success, the world's definition of power and wealth and pursue it, living in endless competition with their neighbors. In this realm, students constantly compete with one another on an endless treadmill of grades, sports, activities, resume building. Employees build "networks" that help them get ahead, but the relationships are mostly transactional. People, activities, studies — none of them are goods in themselves, but are flattened out into means to some other goal. Not that we would ever want to admit to this, of course! It's just a way of living that seems necessary. So, we say, "that's the way the world is," or "that's office politics for you," or "that's the rat race."

Maybe you can think of other ways that we live, ways that seem like living but whose values you really wouldn't want to admit to, ways that are ultimately fruitless from the perspective of hope and love. Maybe you can think of all the reasons that you have used to stay cut off from your neighbors, to hide, the way my Uncle Tom used his diagnosis as a reason not to get to know anyone in his new building. Maybe you don't like to think about these things or admit to them. It's not easy to admit how much we make peace with the ways of spiritual death.

The good news is that today, God will not allow us to stay stuck in these ways! Today, the word of God breaks in: *awake, sleeper, rise from death, and Christ shall give you light.* Real life in Christ, it turns out, is more than mere survival, more than success as the world imagines it, different than the cutthroat ways we assume are just part of life in upper-middle class America. Real life in Christ is righteousness: living with one another in just relationships that bring flourishing to all. Real life in Christ is truthful: it sees things for what they are. Real life in Christ is the love that regards people as fellow creatures of God, that sees community not competition.

Christ is a light which, like daylight in the ancient world, allowed people to see and be seen, a light which exposes the truth about the death-dealing and fruitless ways that we were living, a light which offers a different, more beautiful path. In the light of Christ, the inward focused congregation stops fearing for its survival and opens its doors to see whom in the neighborhood it can bless. In the light of Christ, the student stops seeing life as a competition and instead as a matter of calling: a matter of who God made her to be and how she can serve.

This new life does not come easy: it requires a cross to put the old fruitless ways to death. So, Jesus comes to us. Listen, he said: I have something more in mind for you than mere survival. I have something more in mind for you than what your world calls success. I have something more in mind for you than the self-focus to which you have become accustomed.

Wake up! Leave those foolish ways of living behind you like the wrappings of my body, left behind in the tomb. *Live as children of the light.* Take as your north star the living presence of Jesus. Stand up, unpack the gifts he has given you: the gifts of justice and mercy, the gifts of love and hope. Open your doors, invite in your neighbors, see them as the people that God has made them to be. You no longer have to remain to yourselves. This congregation need not remain to itself, cowering behind its own wooden doors, obsessed by the budgets and challenges of being church in twenty-first-century America.

Christ has died and is risen *for you.* He shines on you so that you can glow with his light. You are no longer dead. So: live!

Amen.

Transformed Lives, Transformed Minds

"You are not in the flesh, you are in the Spirit!" With these words, Romans announced that Christians are a part of an entirely new reality. It is a done deal. Today we get to ponder what it means that we are in the Spirit and the Spirit dwells in us.

Last week, our Ephesians reading prompted us to consider the contrast in our actions, in our deeds, in the ways we live. Today, I believe that our second reading from Romans is inviting to us to consider our mindsets, our thoughts. Last week was about the walk, this week is about the talk. During our waking hours, we are constantly having thoughts and emotions; we perceive the outside world and respond to it; we deliberate and decide. We filter our experiences through our personal values and examine them in the light of our unique experiences; the work of community in large part involves people sharing their minds, coming together either in discovery of common values or across significant differences.

As a new creation in Christ, however, our minds are not just our own, to be set on whatever we choose. Rather, they are set on the things of the Spirit — the Spirit of the living Christ. This life in the Spirit is very different, Romans tell us, than if our minds were set on something else that Romans called "the flesh."

My experience when people read this part of Romans, or hear it read aloud in worship on Sunday, is that their first reaction is, "I have *no* idea what this is all about." Or, as 2 Peter 3:16 says about Paul's letters, "There are some things in them that are hard to understand." And the spirit and flesh distinction is one such thing. For Paul, the flesh is not the physical world, or the bones and muscle that make up our bodies. Rather, for Paul, "flesh" is that dimension of our being that is subject to the rule of sin and evil. Meanwhile, the "Spirit" is the very presence of God. Romans was inviting us to allow our thoughts and feelings, our values and choices, our perceptions of the world around us and our responses to it, to happen in and through the Holy Spirit.

This is, no doubt, still quite abstract so I wanted to share with you an experience of mine that helped me understand the difference between minds that are set on the things of the flesh versus the minds that are set on the things of the Spirit.

I currently pastor a congregation in Butler, Pennsylvania. Prior to July 13, 2024, few people outside of Southwestern Pennsylvania had ever heard of it. In 1940, the Bantam® Jeep was invented here, so sometimes Jeep enthusiasts are acquainted with us, but there aren't major historical sites, tourist attractions, or universities that draw outsiders to the area. For years, when a new acquaintance would ask, "where do you serve?" I would explain, "Oh, about thirty miles north of Pittsburgh."

Then, that July, someone tried, and almost succeeded, to assassinate former President Trump at a rally at the Butler Farm Show grounds a few miles out of town. A rallygoer died protecting his family and suddenly our community was in the media spotlight.

An act of violence has ripple effects through the community, triggering fear and anger, which had been historically high through the 2024 election season. In the weeks that followed the shooting, the owner of several local digital billboards posted signs depicting Kamala Harris with horns as well as messages that seemed to blame Democrats for the assassination attempt (which wasn't true). Local, then national, media reported on tense text message exchanges between county leaders. In a small town, where it seems as though everyone knows everyone and has for their whole lives, reports and signs like these kept the cycle of reactivity and blame going. Who was most at fault for what happened? Who was at for the culture of division and violence?

When these conversations got going — say, in a meeting — my experience was that the purpose of the gathering would be immediately derailed. No new ministry could be planned, decisions made, or new goals set.

I was getting a very good lesson in what Romans means when it talks about "to set the mind on the flesh is death." "The flesh" is self-centered not God-centered, self-serving not neighbor-serving. "The flesh" plays blame games, avoids responsibility, thrives on reactivity. "The flesh" is not particularly interested in what God might think about a situation or a person; it gives not one whit about what God commands. Instead, it has its own opinions and does its own research. It lives by its own ambitions and desires and keeps score with others in an endless competition. It insists that peace between enemies is impossible because it never wants to give up or give in or give away. "The flesh" perceives itself to be locked into an all-out battle for survival.

I suspect that you can name them other times when it seems that our minds are set on the things of the flesh. A family conflict goes on for years with endless litanies of complaints but no real solution. In the office, two employees vie for promotion in ways that make life stressful for everyone else. At the local school board meeting, members of the board rig the rules of order to suit their agenda — and opponents react.

But you are not in the flesh, you are in the spirit! This is the Spirit of the of the one who raised Jesus Christ from death, in whom something brand new has broken into the world. That very spirit now, by the grace of God, has chosen to live in us. I think of the Romans' all-encompassing language. The Spirit dwells in us, opens our hearts to our neighbor's needs, and rewires our brains for new choices. The Spirit focuses our minds to remember that all people are children of God and bear human dignity. The Spirit invites us into confidence that

God holds the future, even when it seems as though the world around us is falling apart. The Spirit assures us that nothing separates us from the love of God in Christ Jesus. To set the mind on the things of the Spirit, therefore, means to discover a source of patience, endurance, and kindness that is not dependent on whatever human situation we find ourselves in. To set our minds on it, Romans tells us, is life and peace.

Back in Butler, when everyone was feeling terrible and angry, I can remember one very hopeful meeting, facilitated by two of my colleagues. One who was known for her progressive views, the other was very conservative. We were trying to plan a prayer vigil and the two of them had very different intuitions about appropriate scripture texts and songs for the occasion. As each difference would arise, they would slow the conversation down and seek to understand the other person's position. At the end, we had an order of service for our vigil that no one would have imagined before, but which we all recognized as a work of the Spirit among us. It was a small moment of peace in an otherwise volatile time, but for me, it represented the possibilities that can emerge when minds are set on the things of the Spirit and when we respond to one another in trust that God is bigger than we are.

The good news for us is that this presence of God, this Spirit into which we may set our minds, is not far off. The Spirit is a present reality for us. We are not in the flesh, Romans assures us, we are in the Spirit. God has made it so, sending the Spirit of his son into our hearts. We are sealed with this Spirit in baptism. We are fed by it in Holy Communion. Because of that, we get to think and hear, feel and respond through its presence.

Amen.

Today There Will Be No Glory

Author's note: In my tradition, the Sunday of the Passion includes a full reading of the appointed gospel account of Jesus' passion, death, and burial. This short sermon is intended to precede that reading rather than follow it.

In his well-known essay, "The God as Teacher and Savior," Søren Kierkegaard told the story of a king who fell in love with a peasant girl. He wanted to live in a true relationship of equality and love with her but found that the chasm between his royalty and her poverty made that impossible. He considered various ways of overcoming the distance between them. He could make her a queen and bring her to his royal palace, blessing her with fine clothing and royal pastimes. This idea he rejected, because she was not a queen and to make her one would be a deception at worst and a diversion at best. In addition, a lover does not require their beloved to change to be worthy of love. So, the king also considered moving to her village, retaining all his power and splendor while being near her. This also he rejected, because while it might impress her, it would not allow them to live as equals. Similarly, he also decided not to show up to in the peasant clothing, for that too would have been a deception; at some point his majesty would shine through the costume.

What could be left for the king to do? What would be left would be for the king to truly to become a peasant, to put aside his royalty and to live alongside his beloved. While true love does not require its beloved to change, it will change itself for the sake of the beloved.

I think of this story whenever I hear the famous hymn from Philippians that is our second reading today. This is a song about Jesus, *who, though he was in the form of God, did not allow equality with God as something to be exploited, but humbled himself ... being born in human likeness.* Make no mistake, when Philippians talks here about the "form" of God and "human likeness," the scripture is not implying that Jesus was a shape-shifting being, appearing divine one day and then human the next. No: what Philippians is telling us is that the Son of God, in great love for us, abandoned the royalty, the glory, the light, the life of heaven and assumed a full human nature. "He became truly human," we confess in the Nicene Creed, with the same kind of body, a mind, feelings, emotions, language, that we all have as human beings. Back in December, on Christmas, we remembered that he had a mother and a birthplace, as babies do. We remember that he was wrapped in swaddling clothes, as human babies are, their bodies not used to the cool temperature outside the womb, their bowels not yet controlled. Truly human.

Today, as we begin Holy Week, we see the outcome of this human life to which he humbled himself. Earlier in our liturgy we told the story of King Jesus, riding into Jerusalem. Rather than the lofty chariot or horse, he chose the donkey, the sign of humble kingship. In accepting true humanity, he did not even insist on the very best human life could offer. In a few moments, we will once again read the drama of his passion, and how he was obedient, as Philippians told us, to the point of death, even death on a cross.

In our sinful world, this is how the king truly comes to us, his beloved. This is the story of how he really takes on our likeness, our form, our condition, our reality. Let me suggest that in a way, there is nothing to see in this story of the passion that you cannot find happening to other human beings in our death-dealing world. He was rejected. He was a victim of indifference and cruelty and ambition and injustice. He was tortured. He grieved in Gethsemane. He felt the full force of abandonment on the cross. He was killed. This was not an act, as if Jesus were just God in disguise, a king in a peasant cloak, only appearing to suffer as we do. There were no miracles here, no angels hiding just behind the curtain to save him at the moment it became too much. He suffered. He died. This is how God comes in love us, for this world of evil and sin and death is where we live.

He lived a full and complete human life, from swaddling clothes to graveclothes, from manger to the tomb. The surprise, to our minds, is that this completely human life completely reveals who God is. This is the paradox: that in humbling himself, Jesus showed us what God's true majesty is like; in taking the position of a servant, he revealed true power. God said "yes," to his obedience and raised him from death. God gave him the name that is above every name. Now at God's right hand, he rules us, true God and true human being that he still is.

In time, we will join him as his beloved. Unlike Kierkegaard's peasant girl that would be made queen simply by the declaration of the king, however, this joining will not be a deception, not a fiction. We will truly belong with our beloved, because he has truly first joined us. The final stanza of a hymn frequently sung in my congregation on Palm Sunday says it well:

> Of death I am no more afraid;
> your dying is my living.
> You clothe me in your royal robes
> that you are always giving.
> Your love is dress enough for me
> to wear through all eternity
> before the throne of heaven,
> where we shall stand close by your side,
> Your church the well-appointed bride,
> When all the faithful gather.[2]

Amen.

Maundy Thursday

2   Paul Gerhardt, "A Lamb Goes Uncomplaining Forth," tr. *Lutheran Book of Worship*, alt. *Evangelical Lutheran Worship* (Minneapolis: Augsburg Fortress, 2006) #340.

1 Corinthians 11:23-26

One Death, One Bread, One Body

"As often as we eat of this bread and drink from this cup, we proclaim the Lord's death until he comes." We proclaim the cross in every celebration of communion, but on Maundy Thursday we especially attend to the connection between his death and this meal. In my church's tradition, the Maundy Thursday liturgy begins by remembering the warmth of Jesus' last supper: the gathering of friends, the sharing of food, the washing of feet, the command to love and serve. It also recalls the cold reality of betrayal by one who gathered with him and his arrest in the garden. After communion is celebrated, the members of our altar guild take to the sacristy the banners, the candlesticks, the altar book and pulpit Bible. The plants that normally fill the chancel with life head out the back door. Then the women remove the paraments. Anything bright and shiny that cannot be moved — the brass cross of the baptismal font — is covered with a black cloth, so that the congregation can sit in the sanctuary for a few minutes in silence without any visual adornment.

The stripping of the altar recalls the way Jesus took off his robe to wash feet at his last supper and the way the soldiers stripped him for crucifixion. His humble service at the supper interprets the meaning of his cross. The cross reveals the depths to which God will go to draw all people to himself in a community of love, self-giving, and mutual care. To death Christ went to wipe out the walls that divide people, the ways of privilege and status, the ways even of sin and shame. In our liturgy, during the eucharistic prayer, the presiding minister declares the words from First Corinthians: "as often as we eat

39

of this bread and drink from this cup, we proclaim the Lord's death until he comes." The congregation roars back, "Christ has died, Christ has risen, Christ will come again." Their response articulates promise and hope. The way of the cross is the way of life; the way of service is the true wealth; the way of forgiveness is the way of true community. We have seen Christ, we see him now, we will see him again.

But we forget him, of course, as the church always has. When Saint Paul wrote to the Corinthian church to remind them of the practice, as of first importance, the urgency came because the church's practice did not match its proclamation; it did not walk its talk. Unlike our churches, which celebrate communion with bread and cup, the earliest churches gathered over a full meal. But Paul had heard some distressing things about the Corinthians' practice. Rather than gathering as a community, the wealthy had good seats and good food; the poorer members, meanwhile, subsisted on scraps. Paul was aghast that the church would allow such social distinctions to survive Jesus' crucifixion. Listen, he said, "I told you the story! As often as you eat of the bread and drink from the cup, you are talking about Jesus' death!" In a passage that is not included in our reading, Paul also warned that eating and drinking unworthily — which I imagine to mean, without reckoning with the death this meal costs — will result in eating and drinking to our own judgment.

This is theology in the key of a warning, which is not popular in most mainline churches these days. I know it's not popular in my own context! But on the night in which Jesus was betrayed, in which he faced down the pangs of hell, I think we can shelve our own discomfort for the moment. Ask: who is here, and who is not, and why? What invisible barriers keep us from one another? And how can those barriers be overcome so that more people can taste and see that God is good, can taste and see how this death brings new life?

One year our congregation's confirmation class consisted of two highly energetic boys, both aged twelve. Because the class was small and the boys committed, our confirmation leaders decided this was an opportunity to experiment with instruction. That summer we swapped traditional classroom instruction for a VBS-like week we called. "Sacrament Camp." We explored what our catechism calls "the gifts and benefits of baptism" by swimming in every swimming pool or lake we could find in our county. For holy communion, we baked bread, visited a vineyard, and toured a wine-making operation (specially designed for the occasion, with no tasting, of course). We also went to many places where communion ministers bring the sacrament to those who cannot make the Sunday morning gathering. We piled in the car and went to a nursing home and brought communion to a homebound member. We strapped on hiking books and walked up the hill to the local hospital and then down the hill and over three blocks to the county jail. Because our city has war memorials, we also stopped at them, a symbolic stop on our pilgrimage, to remember how chaplains in the military also celebrate communion wherever the military is deployed.

By design, the experiment got us out of the building, which was where the boys had most of their experience with sacraments. When Jesus gave his disciples bread and wine on the night before his death and commanded that we remember him every time we "do this," he did not confine the practice to a place. The church is made of living stones; it is not a building of quarried rock. It is always worth wondering who is hungry.

A mere seven months after sacrament camp ended, the pandemic of 2020 began. Like many congregations, we worshiped online only for a while, which was how we learned that some of our most regular Sunday morning attendees had no internet access or technological knowledge. They worshiped with us in spirit, using printed bulletins the church office sent out. During that time, there was a great deal of discussion within our denomination about "zoom communion," and some congregations began the practice. But for us, the practice was nonstarter. Celebrating communion in a way in which a sizeable portion of our congregation did not have access was a nonstarter. The practice of visiting — in homes, hospitals, prisons, nursing facilities, the practice which normally connected those who could make the 10 am worship service with those who could not — was not available to us. Recognizing that we were all homebound by the power of death at work in the pandemic, we did *not* eat of the bread and we did *not* drink of the cup and so we proclaimed the death of the one whose death unites us.

The experience heightened our awareness of the barriers that have always existed, but had become part of the furniture. It is always worth wondering who is hungry. It is also worth wondering who, because they have not been fed, has forgotten that such food exists, who does not know that such food and its mercy is for them: those who were, from our tradition's perspective, considered too young. Those who, because of the demands of a 24-hour economy, had to work. Those whose brain chemistry or mental health made it hard to sit still or be seen by others. Those for whom our denomination's by-the-book liturgical language was a few grade levels beyond accessible. During the pandemic, "normal" was stripped away like paraments on Maundy Thursday and so was our understanding that the way we had been doing things was the way things had to be.

Not ourselves, or the ways we have always done things; not who is always here, but Christ is proclaimed, and here proclaimed is his death. His death, which puts to death all our divisions. His blood which makes of different people one new humanity. His life, by which the teacher and master becomes a servant and by which disciples become servants and all become friends. His promise to come again: here in this place, here in this bread, here in the warmth of this evening.

Proclaim it: Christ has died, Christ has risen, Christ will come again.

Amen.

He Was Not Saved

When human beings are faced with a death too-soon, loud cries and tears are what happens. I once knew a man who had served in the German navy during the Second World War. After surviving the torpedoing of his ship and a stint as a prisoner of war, he ultimately came to the United States as a refugee. I got to know him during the last years of his life, when busyness and work could no longer quiet the memories he held of his shipmates, fighting for their lives in the swirling waters as the ship sank, crying for their mothers, *"Mutti! Hilfe! Mother! Help!"* The enemy navy vessel saved as many as they could, making them prisoners of war.

Jesus cried. The gospel of John doesn't record it, but the other gospel writers do: the anguish in Gethsemane — "let this cup pass;" the dereliction on the cross, "My God, my God, why have you forsaken me?" In the days of his flesh, Hebrews tells us, "Jesus offered up loud cries and tears to the one who was able to save him from death."

He cried to God who could save him from death. But his reverent submission earned him only a hearing. He cried and was heard. He was heard, but he was not saved. God could have saved him but did not. Tonight, on Good Friday, we ponder this divine inactivity, we sit with God's stillness and Jesus' obedience. God's arm is not too short to save, but God does not reach out; God's might is hidden and but revealed instead are the ways of human beings. The betrayal of Judas, the jealousy of the high priests, the cynicism and ambition of Pilate, the cruelty of the soldiers, the fear of the disciples, the rage of the crowd — any of those things alone could elicit loud cries and tears; together they result in his death. On Good Friday, God is still and lets our human rejection of God be what it is. God could save him but did not, so that we get a picture of what is to live without God. We do not have to wait for some far-off day for judgment: this day will tell us we need to know about the depth of human sin.

In the haunting "Terce" movement of his poem "Horae Canonicae," W.H. Auden portrayed Good Friday as the inexorable result of people simply going about their lives and doing their duties as assigned. Focused on their own small sliver of responsibility and distracted by their personal concerns, amusements, and gossip, the hangman, the judge, the poet, and the professionals of the modern city all miss the big picture. God is absent, and so, Auden noted, "each of us / prays to an image of an image of himself." They remain unaware of their complicity in the drama of death. Only their victim sees the big picture, knows that on this day "That not one of us will slip up / that the machinery of our world / will function without a hitch... / knows that by sundown / we shall have had a Good Friday."

This machinery of the world leads to the cross, and not only to Jesus' cross, but to the many places where there are loud cries and tears that go unheard by those who could help. I think of the victims of war who now call out for their mothers — in Arabic, in Hebrew, in Ukrainian, and in Russian, in the many indigenous languages of Sudan. I think of children in our own country who cower under desks or in corners while practicing lockdowns, knowing that there may be a day when it will not be practice, when they will text their fathers, their mothers, "There are gunshots. Please know I love you." I think of how many white folks in this nation have a hard time hearing the truth about the racism of our past and therefore have a hard time even listening to those who have been harmed the most by that history, much less changing for the sake of justice. This is the machinery of our unrepentant world — how it crushes people, how it thrives on indifference, how it prefers what it calls "power" to God's goodness, how quick it is to exchange the life that God wants for us for death. On Good Friday, as God is still, we sit with the cross and all it tells us.

But the good news is that Good Friday is not the end of the story. We do not celebrate Good Friday on its own but always as a part of the great drama of Holy Week and Easter. God, who did not save Jesus on Friday, raised him on Sunday to greater glory, to what Hebrews calls "perfection." Forty days later, God seated him at God's right hand, where he now rules all of creation and where he serves, Hebrews tells us, as a great high priest. What do priests do? For many of us Christians, the Jewish image of the "high priest" is completely foreign. For Protestants, the idea of *any* priest — high, Jewish, Christian, or otherwise — may be even more so.

For tonight, let us simply describe the role of the priest simply: priests pray for others. They mediate between God and the people, interpreting one to the other. They are go-betweens, keeping the two parties connected. Now risen from death and ascended on high, Jesus carries with him into heaven the flesh that bore the nails and the crown of thorns. In heaven, he is both the risen Lord who was made perfect in resurrection but also the obedient Son who was not saved on Friday. By his cross, he connects a world that is often satisfied to live without God with God, the true source of its life.

It is in this way that he can really help us, not from a pedestal above us but as one who knows what it is to live and suffer in a world that forgets its God. Now, as priest, he continually prays. He prays for those slaughtered in war, the schoolchildren behind locked-down doors, the bearers of every historical trauma. He prays for Auden's hangman, the judge, the poet, the professionals, the indifferent ones who just want to go about their business, those of us who don't want to think too deeply about our part in the machinery of death. He prays, because he knows, with loud cries and tears: Father! Father! Save them! Help!

Amen.

God Allows
Him To Appear

Alleluia, Christ is risen! He is risen indeed.

Today, we are here to take our parts in God's cosmic joke on sin and the grave. Hence the flowers and the trumpet and the candy. Jesus Christ has been raised from the dead, and death no longer has dominion over him.

In a few hours, the shine of the holiday will be off. The little girls will trade their dresses for play clothes, the candy will be unwrapped, and the lilies will bow their heads. We'll look at our calendars to see this week's appointments, although some of us will not need a calendar to tell us that a biopsy or a scan is on the agenda. We'll open the newspapers tomorrow to read all the in-depth reporting on what the powers of sin and death have done this week. Christ is risen, he is risen indeed, but the thread that connects his resurrection and our reality can sometimes seem so fragile.

When I was a child, I can remember sitting in church one Sunday coloring a picture the usher gave me of the story: a cave with a stone rolled away, the women, and the two dazzling men. This, I thought, doesn't make much sense. The previous week's handout from the usher had been a connect-the-dots activity that ultimately (after drawing the lines in the right order) depicted Jesus standing before Pilate. This got me thinking. Wouldn't it have made more sense for Jesus, upon rising, to go back to the places where he had been condemned? Wouldn't it have been a better show if he had shown up at Pilate's palace to swagger before the soldiers so as to say, "Boys, did you ever make a big mistake!" Why did he choose the women when he could have made his case so much more convincingly?

Wouldn't it be great if Jesus could appear in fuller, clearer terms to people we would wish to believe in him, or in places that really could use a jolt of life. Why not the chemo clinic, where he can rock the hell out of the recliners and the IV poles and the televisions perennially set to the home and garden network? Why does he not appear to — oh, I don't know — your brother or your kids, to convince them that the golden rule is a good idea and should be followed, and by the way, you'd really like to be repaid those thousand dollars they owe you. Why can he not go to those who seem unmistakably in the grip of the powers of death, the KKK, those who plan for terror or war? Wouldn't it be great if he would appear in an unmistakable way to those folks and say, "Greetings, gentlemen, there are some things you need to reconsider!" Wouldn't *that* make Easter make so much more sense?

As it is, the way the story goes, when the resurrection happened, there was not a demonstration to those whom we might think might need a dose of glory to get the truth. Instead, there was a small group of women who saw two men and the stone rolled away. According to the gospel of Luke, the disciples didn't even believe *them*, thinking all they said was an idle tale. Peter went later and saw the cloths — just the cloths, by themselves. It was not, you might say, a promising start.

But it *was* a start. Our second reading, from Acts, connects the dots from Jesus' resurrection to what happened later in Peter's life. For Peter, seeing those cloths was the beginning of believing that there was something more than death. Later, he had an experience of Christ as raised from the dead. And according to him, it happened, not in an stunning display of power and proof, but in an ordinary meal. Hear again how he described it in Acts 10, our Second Lesson, "They put him to death by hanging him on a tree, but God raised him on the third day and allowed him to appear, *not to all the people*, but to those who were chosen by God as witnesses, and who ate and drank with him after he rose from the dead."

Not to all the people, but to those who ate and drank with him after he rose from the dead. Not to *all,* but to those. Not to those whom we most wish would "get it," but us, who perhaps need to "get it" more than we realize. The stunning good news of resurrection never starts with an overwhelming display of power that everyone can see. It starts with a few who see the cloths, the men, and the stone.

God, it seems, has never needed the whole world to be one hundred percent convinced of Jesus' resurrection in order for his risen life to give us power for a new kind of living. God has used small things, just glimpses, like linen cloths rolled up by themselves, like an angel's act of sitting on a stone, to break the good news of resurrection into the world. God has always used witnesses like Peter, who are as ordinary as you and me. Witnesses hear the news and tell the story of all they have seen and heard, and it is through the witnesses that the word gets out that God has something more in mind than death. Through their testimony a brand-new reality comes into focus and becomes a possibility in the lives of people in the here and now. Can you remember all the times that a story gave you hope? A story in which life overcame death or in which love overcame hatred? Can you remember how it lit something new within you or sparked your imagination? This is the story of God that Peter told; this is the story that we are sent to tell.

The line that connects the dots between his resurrection and our daily lives is his grace at work in us. Today, that grace is made delivered, made real, in bread and wine, in Christ's body and blood. Here, you do get to be the one who eats and drinks with him after he rose from the dead. Here, at his table, he welcomes you again with bread and wine. Here he chooses you as a witness. He gives you this story: They put him to death on a tree, but God raised him up. What a world locked in hopelessness and despair needs is are witnesses, people carrying the story with them. Hospital rooms, our classrooms, our streets, and our homes all are in desperate need of people who say, "The Lord is risen, he is risen indeed."

Amen.

Second Sunday of Easter
1 Peter 1:3-9

God Is In Charge Of Our Hope

The members of Pilgrim Presbyterian Church hosted a community meal every Monday evening in their church's basement. Free to all comers, the meals were usually simple: casserole and bread, chili and cornbread, sloppy joes. The kitchen was small and the needs of the community large, and so the cooks did not let things get too complicated.

Then one Holy Week, a generous donor called the church and offered them twenty hams for Easter Monday. "Well, we *should* have an Easter feast" the planning team quickly decided. Starting early on Monday morning, they worked in shifts to prepare the sides: coleslaw, baked beans, mac and cheese, rolls and butter. A crafty volunteer even arranged centerpieces for the tables. Everything was ready for the community to have an Easter feast. The team hoped that the experience would be celebratory for everyone.

Their hopes were dashed ten minutes after the doors opened. Darren, a regular, seemed not to have taken his medications for a few days, and his temper was quickly triggered when someone touched him on the shoulder and asked him to move with the line. A punch was thrown. Jane, who knew Darren from her many Mondays welcoming people, tried to step in and got elbowed in the face. A few diners became frightened and started to leave. In the fray, at least one centerpiece crashed to the ground and shattered. Though later things calmed down and people ate, disappointment hung heavy in the air. The joyfulness of Easter seemed to have been eclipsed by human brokenness.

Last week, with Christians throughout the world, we celebrated our tradition's biggest feast. Depending on where you worshiped, there may have been brass quartets and choir processions or fog machines and flashing lights, flowered crosses and altar flowers or the most splendid visuals for the screen displays. Most congregations give Easter their very best, all to proclaim the good news that Christ is risen.

Then Easter Monday came. On Easter Sunday, we celebrated God's cosmic joke on death. On Easter Monday, we opened our newspapers or our news apps to discover death's ongoing grip on the world in war and violence. On Sunday, we set our mind on the things that are above, where Christ is. On Monday, we set our minds on our calendars, with their doctor's appointments and court dates and with the meetings that make the things below work. Our experience of Easter can seem fragile in the face of all that flies in the face of hope.

That is why it is good on this second Sunday of Easter to gather once again and hear the news that we are not in charge of our own hope. Rather, *God* gives us a new birth into a living hope, our reading from 1 Peter tells us. Moreover, this hope is not limited by our feelings, our plans, or our experience, which go up and down and change from day to day. Our hope's object is Jesus himself and the salvation that he has given us in his death and resurrection. He holds our future, and nothing can take that away, because it is kept safe in God's hands. This, our text tells us, is our inheritance in heaven. This salvation cannot get the wind knocked out of it at Easter dinner. This salvation will not shatter to the ground like a vase. This salvation will not wear out like a garment over time or rot like old food. It is "imperishable, undefiled, and unfading;" it is kept in heaven where sin and death have no power to destroy.

The people who first heard the words of 1 Peter lived, as we will see over the coming weeks, in a time of persecution and rejection. They suffered "various trials," which would test their faith. But 1 Peter's people had also, alongside all of those trials, discovered a curious thing. Even though they couldn't always see or feel the new creation Christ had promised them in the present moment, the promise of heaven was still there, as though hidden behind a curtain, separated from their lives by a thin veil. The promise, however, was no less real for being hidden.

Although each day might bring family fights with unbelieving relatives, or accusations in court, or the hostility of their neighbors, none of these struggles could diminish God's future. This discovery, this sense of grace, was so counter to expectation, so counter to experience, that it could be none other than the work of God. God's ongoing work to secure this solid future was an occasion for rejoicing. "Even though you do not see him, you love him, and even though you do not see him now, you believe in him and rejoice with an indescribable and glorious joy."

I think these words were left for us as scripture as a word from God to summon us into that same kind of hope. Yes, it is a week after Easter. Yes, the flowers have faded, and the choir may have the Sunday off; the festivals are over, and we are "back to normal." The injustices of life in this world may have reared their ugly heads many times in the last week. For so many reasons, hope can be hard to feel. So let the word of God invite you to sit with 1 Peter's people, and into their confidence that reality is bigger than what we can see and what we can feel. For God is bigger than what we can see and what we can feel. Here is the horizon of our hope: Jesus is risen. The grave could not hold him. His risen presence is the future. He is *your* future. He reigns at God's right hand in heaven and so he fills all of creation. Sometimes we cannot see him through our various trials. Still, friends, take heart, because he sees you and he is present with you even when you do not know it.

Back at Pilgrim Presbyterian church, on the Easter Tuesday after the Easter Monday when the planned feast seemed to dissolve in disorder, the community dinner planning team gathered. They processed their experience with Darren and the fist fight and checked in on Jane. Then Ricardo spoke up: you know, despite all of this, I saw some signs of grace. There was a little girl who was so excited about the mac and cheese she asked for seconds. Her grandmother had brought her and thanked us for a good Easter. Slowly, the team recounted other signs of grace: "You know who made the coleslaw? Angela. She did it at home. She can't get in the kitchen with her walker when everyone is here, but she was glad to be able to contribute. As the thanksgivings grew in number, the team decided that despite the fight, the feast was worth doing again next year. After all, Jesus is risen. "Isn't that why we are here?" someone asked.

Indeed.

Amen.

Third Sunday of Easter
1 Peter 1:17-23

Free From Futile Family Habits

"In baptism our gracious heavenly Father frees us from sin and death by joining us to the death and resurrection of our Lord Jesus Christ." So read the opening words of the baptismal liturgy in my church's worship resource, *Evangelical Lutheran Worship*. The service continues, "We are born children of a fallen humanity; by water and the Holy Spirit we are reborn children of God and made members of the church, the body of Christ. Living with Christ in the communion of saints, we grow in faith, hope, and obedience to the will of God."

I don't know how things are for you in your congregation, but most of the baptisms I get to lead are of babies or small children, who usually are brought to the baptismal font by their parents and surrounded by grandparents, great-grandparents, and sponsors. When I proclaim the opening words of the baptismal rite, I'm always struck by how small the baby is, and how big the drama of the sacrament is. By water and word, Christ takes the baptized from sin to forgiveness, from living for oneself to living in community, from being without God to being with God, from death to life. By water and the enduring word of God, the baptized are born anew. Only faith can grasp such a thing; it hardly makes sense to our minds. Why does such a little person — who still often has that new baby smell — need such a new birth?

In addition to these dramatic changes, our second reading, from 1 Peter, introduces us to another kind of change brought about by life in Christ. To be born anew in Christ, our scripture tells us, means that we are redeemed, or set free, "from the futile ways that [we] inherited from our ancestors." Try announcing that to a family of four generations, gathered around a font: "Guess what, little one! Now we are going to set you free from your family's senseless teachings." That would sound even more dramatic, more radical, than the already enormous changes announced in the baptismal liturgy as it is. I could even imagine it sounding offensive to some.

So, let's go there. How is it that the baptized life, the Easter life in Christ, leads us to break with the futile ways inherited by our ancestors? How is that break good news?

The early Christians who heard these words first would have understood their meaning. After all, they were *not* babies who had been carried by their parents to the baptismal font. They did not learn Bible stories while sitting on their grandparents' laps or tag along with their cousins to vacation Bible school. These folks who heard 1 Peter had quite literally been called away from the pagan religion that surrounded them. They no longer worshiped its idols, participated in its sacrifices, and reveled in the splendor of its festivals. They gave up on their ancestors' fascination with spectacle and honor and position and wealth. In exchange they opted for the values of humility and mutual love. They put all their trust in an unseen God revealed in a crucified Jewish man from Palestine, which was something that their neighbors especially could not understand: *"You worship a God who embraced a cross?"* Crucifixion was the most shameful and humiliating kind of death that there was!

But those who worshiped this God discovered a strange thing.

Those who worshiped this God discovered that the blood of Jesus seemed to bring a kind of life and hope that idols never brought.

Those who found their life in the blood of Jesus discovered that humility and mutual love brought a kind of wealth that silver and gold could not.

Those who practiced humility and mutual love discovered a hope more enduring than a temple made by human hands.

Those who were born anew in Christ discovered that their former way of life, the way of life their ancestors had always known — their inherited values, traditions, customs, and practices — all these were just exercises in futility.

Now, for many of us, Christ's invitation to new life in him does not seem to us to be as clear a break with our family, our ancestors, or our culture as it was to 1 Peter's people. Some (though not all!) of us count our ancestors as our most important faith influences. And in some parts of our country communal patterns of life are shaped by centuries of Christian dominance: Christian holidays off from school, Sunday mornings still somewhat protected, Christian prayer practiced in public space. This is beginning to change in some places, and Christians are starting to experience more and more of twenty-first-century life as a kind of "exile," similar to the early church. But still, for most of us, family and faith and culture have gone together.

But even within this framework, there are still "ways of life" that are, from the perspective of life in Christ, "futile." That is to say, there are ways of life that don't get us anywhere, that aren't all that life-giving.

For example, I think of how we baptize babies and then allow them to grow up thinking that they are not worthy of as much love because of how they look, or because of their weight, or because of the color of their skin or the texture of their hair. Thus, the baptismal promise — that we are created by God, made worthy in Christ, called to grow up in Christ and to serve — is submerged. Many adult women, I know, still struggle to believe that they are lovable as they are — they believe that they would be much more lovable if only they were ten pounds lighter and their skin just a smidge tighter.

You have been redeemed from this, by the blood of Christ, not with another diet plan or another anti-aging regimen but by the very life of Christ! And with that, your hope, your peace, your trust is in God!

Another example: I have served in majority white contexts for most of my ministry. Many members of these churches remember being brought to church by their "ancestors." But they also remember ways that their parents and their grandparents tolerated cruel and casual forms of racism that have infected our culture and dealt death to people of color. They have had to learn — sometimes painfully — that God in Christ calls them to a different way, that Christ not only releases them from their ancestors' prejudices and their hateful practices, but actively calls them to seek justice and healing. What they have discovered, though, is that this way of Christ is more life-giving than the racist patterns that promised privilege but really only brought death. Set free from the past and set free for Christ, these people have discovered that it is much more joyful to love, rather than to hate, to accept, rather than to fear, and foster communities where people seek mutual trust and accountability rather than domination.

There are many such values in our culture that are incompatible with life in Christ, that cannot withstand the baptism into his death. Sometimes those very values are held by the people who stand around the baptismal fonts. Sometimes, they are patterns of life hidden within the families, hard to see on Sunday morning.

The good news is this: *you were ransomed from the futile ways inherited by your ancestors, not with silver or gold but by the precious blood of Christ.* God intends for us the same hope and peace, the same humility and mutual love that God intended for the people who first heard 1 Peter. God intends for us know true life by knowing a crucified man from Palestine. God intends for us to know a peace in our very being that comes from God alone. This life cannot be earned by a diet and exercise program. This life will never be found in systems of oppression and degradation. It can only be received as a gift of love, at the hands of the crucified Jesus, in water that washes over us as infants, as children, as adults — bringing us from death to life.

Amen.

Alive In Christ And Suffering For Faith

There are some dangers in this text we have for our second reading — maybe not in the text itself, but in the ways that we often have heard and interpreted and applied these words to our lives. This passage addresses the experience, all too common and real in our fallen world, of being on the receiving end of abuse and physical violence. It commends the virtue of "endurance" while receiving such treatment. In some Christian traditions, such words have been used to silence abused spouses (particularly women) and to valorize their suffering as being a kind of Christ-like self-offering. In the history of our nation, this passage — which, in its wider context, addresses how believing slaves should live — has been used to justify the enslavement and oppression of people of color. Although such interpretations have fallen out of favor in most mainline churches, some of us still hear this text as God saying that unjust suffering is commendable and that we should endure it at all costs. To do so, we hear, is Christ-like, for Jesus himself suffered.

Before we get further, I want to declare that to hear this text in such ways is death-dealing. Those who use it in such ways are ministers of death and not proclaimers of good news. In Jesus is "life." He is God's victory over evil and not its validation. Before we can figure out what it means to have his suffering as an example, we have to be clear that God's ultimate will for us is freedom from abuse and liberation from injustice. God does not want people to be trapped in violent homes. God does not consign people to subservient social standing. Since today is often called "Good Shepherd Sunday," it might be helpful to think of this passage in the light of what it means to have Jesus as a good shepherd. A good shepherd does not allow the animals of the flock to wound one another. A good shepherd works to keep her sheep free from predators and hazards. Jesus, our good shepherd, has even laid down his life for the sheep. He has done this not so that we can further suffer, but so that, 1 Peter said, "we can live for righteousness." That is what God wants for us: that we live.

With that in mind, how are we to understand the challenging word that 1 Peter gives us, that Christ's suffering is to be an example for us? The first thing to note is that in this passage is primarily talking about the kind of suffering in which one can give witness to one's Christian faith. We'll encounter this idea a bit more in the weeks to come. The primary situation of suffering that 1 Peter has in mind is the suffering that is endured because one chooses to follow Christ and because one has come to believe that the new creation he is bringing about is deep, rich, and life-giving. In the face of God's new creation, the powers of sin and death squeal because their time is short in the face of God's promise; those powers push back and make life hard for faithful people. That's the kind of suffering 1 Peter hopes we will endure: suffering for the sake of faith. That's a qualitatively different kind of suffering than the suffering endured because someone just needs to have power over us. That's the first thing to note.

The second thing to notice is that within this context of suffering for faith, the thing that 1 Peter seems to be most concerned about is how we respond to attack — with controlling that which is in our power to control. He is not saying, "Let them hit you as often as they want to hit you!" because that, again, would be a word of death and not the gospel of life. He was saying, "Don't return abuse for abuse. Do not engage in evil talk or deeds yourselves." As anyone who has ever been called a name knows, however, that is very hard to do!

It is, however, what Jesus did for us, and it is how God, in Christ, brought a new creation into the world. The powers that dominate the old creation, the powers of sin, run on an endless cycle of tit-for-tat, of an eye for an eye. The powers of sin run on revenge and believe that what goes around, comes around. Jesus did not live in this way. He did not return abuse for abuse. He did not raise his hackles when threatened. If he had lowered himself to the level of his abusers, it might have been understandable, but nothing would have changed for us. In absorbing the cruelty that was inflicted on him without returning it, he disarmed the powers of evil and demonstrated that they had no hold over him. This is how he can help us. This is how his grace broke into the world, and this is it breaks in now as people choose to trust in his grace. Suffering for the sake of faith is possible, 1 Peter thinks, because it participates in the life that Christ has gained for us through his death and life.

The late Georgia congressman and civil rights activists John Lewis famously said that to achieve change, it was important to get into "good trouble; necessary trouble." He said this at the time he was helping to organize bus boycotts and sit-ins at segregated lunch counters in the American south. At the same time, he learned the strategies of non-violent resistance, to which he was committed until he died in 2020. He learned how to be beaten without hitting back, how to be called names without calling names in return. To do that required suffering: Lewis recalled nearly dying at one point during the Freedom Rides into the deep South. At the same time, however, Lewis was doing this for the sake of life — to turn back the tide of terror and oppression that denied the human dignity of black people across the nation and especially in segregated states. This, I think, is the kind of suffering that 1 Peter commends: the suffering that tells a greater story about God's ultimate will for life, suffering that does not return evil for evil, suffering that trusts the good shepherd.

Amen.

Fifth Sunday of Easter
1 Peter 2:2-10

He Chooses Us

In her lovely book, *Grace (Eventually): Thoughts on Faith,* Anne Lamott described "Loved and Chosen," an activity that she did every Sunday with a children's class at her church. She would sit on the couch in their classroom and deliberately invite kids wearing a particular outfit to come and sit with her: "Is anyone here wearing a blue sweatshirt with Pokémon on it?" she would ask. "The four-year old looked down at his chest, astonished to discover that he matched this description — like, what are the odds? He raised his hand. 'Come over here to the couch,' I said. You are so loved, so chosen."[3]

So it went for all of the children in the class.

Today, I want to invite you into the surprise and the joy of that four-year old, for God has loved and chosen you. Our text from 1 Peter said it plainly: You are a chosen race, a royal priesthood, a holy nation, God's own people, in order that you may proclaim the mighty acts of him who brought you out of darkness into his own marvelous light."

Maybe you are astonished to discover that you fit the description. I can certainly say that on any given day I feel my life is too messy to be considered "royal," and my relationships too broken to qualify as "holy." Most of us have reasons for why we should not qualify for these descriptors. Still, God has looked inside each one of us; God knows the hairs on our heads and knows us better than we know ourselves. God knows our gifts and our failings, our greatest successes and our deepest, most miserable failures. God knows all of these things and chose us. God sent Jesus Christ to die and rise for each one of you — and

3   Anne Lamott, *Grace (Eventually): Thoughts on Faith,* New York: Riverhead, 2007. *p. 29*

for me. Now alive and in the power of the Spirit, Christ draws us together as a new people, a household of living stones, the delightful people of God. Together, we get to do the hopeful work of talking like Jesus, following Jesus, loving our neighbors, and celebrating in all that we do his marvelous life. We get to do this, because God has loved and chosen us first.

This joyful image of being chosen, though, is not always how God's decision making is portrayed. Some years ago, a famous radio preacher named Harold Camping regularly stirred folks with his predictions about the end of the world — and his predictions about who would be chosen to be saved. Camping famously claimed that all churches were apostate and that no one who was a member of a church would go to heaven. He got a lot of press and became the butt of many jokes.

When I listened to people talk about him, though, I realized that even if people thought his predictions were hogwash, they often shared his picture of God as a God who chooses up sides. This God is picking an A team to go to heaven and a B team to go to hell, picking winners, who meet the Lord in the air and losers, who experience tribulation on earth. As part of that theological picture, Christians have to be at work constantly to merit God's choice, have to prove that we are living right, that we are worthy.

That is why, I think, it is so important to hear again the news from the scriptures today of how God chooses. God chooses for the lost, the least, and the last. Why? Because the choice of God is, first and foremost, a choice for Jesus Christ. 1 Peter compares Jesus to a stone that the builders threw out in their building project. His message was rejected by his people. He was sentenced to death. Hanging on the cross, he was literally "left behind" — as his friends deserted him and fled.

And yet, the scripture declares, God has made that stone the builders rejected into the chief cornerstone. God said "yes" to the one who lost it all on the cross; "yes" to the one who died a sinner's death; "yes" to the one who was judged. "Yes" to the way he lived and "yes" to the way he died. God declared, in the end, that Jesus was the way — the way that God was coming to us. The one reliable way we have to know what the Father is like is to look at Jesus, and it's there that we see how deeply God is *for* us; how deeply we are loved and chosen.

What does that mean for those who do not recognize him as the way? What about those who don't believe, or who believe in something else — like Islam, or Buddhism? What happens if you reject Jesus? What happens if someone never hears? Truthfully, we cannot say. It's not our concern. This impulse that goes on in our culture about who's in heaven and who's in hell says more about our own desire to be God-like than it does about the eternal destiny of anyone. Frankly, I also think that our impulse to judgementalism is why we are so harshly critical of ourselves, why we hear words like "you are a chosen race, a royal priesthood, a holy nation" and think, "that can't possibly be me!" or "anyone who thinks that my church is 'holy' doesn't know some of my fellow church members!"

As for me, I have hope and faith that the God who raised Jesus from the dead will make a way for everyone, even those who die without cleaning up from major messes that they make, because God continues to make a way to me despite the messes that I have made. Death is not the last word for our God. God has the knowledge and the skills to forgive those who have messed up, reconcile people to each other, and welcome everyone home.

Not one of us could have made the choice *for* God. Not one of us could have accepted the news about God. Rather, God has accepted us. God has chosen *for us*. And this is the very definition of grace: to live in the presence of one who is always *for you*.

Some years ago, I went on a silent retreat. The only words spoken during the day came at the end of the evening prayer time, after retreatants sat for a quiet hour in the chapel together. One night, the retreat leader ended the prayer by saying, "Lord, help us to believe the truth about ourselves, no matter how beautiful it is."

Loving God, help us to believe this beautiful truth, that we are loved and chosen.

Amen.

The Strife Is Over, The Battle Won

Last week, looking at 1 Peter, we heard the marvelous declaration that in Jesus Christ, we are a chosen race, a royal priesthood, a holy nation. We are God's people, loved and chosen. It is a beautiful truth!

Living as God's people, however, does not always *feel* very beautiful. God's love for us is not a guarantee that people will always treat us with respect and kindness. The world around us may have never heard that love is at the heart of the universe, at the heart of our very existence. Or, it may have forgotten. A world that does not know that it is loved can be very unloving. Thus, in our daily lives we can bump into a lot of unloving behavior. Sometimes our faith can become fodder for people to make fun of us. Sometimes, we can be tempted to respond in kind, with insults for insults.

Our reading from 1 Peter today has a word that addresses us when we are in this situation. It's a complex passage, with some very dense biblical and theological references. I'll say more about those in a minute. The passage starts out, however, by telling us to be who we are in Christ. In the face of an unloving world, 1 Peter says, hold on to those things that characterize a loved and chosen existence. Hold on, in your hearts, to Christ as Lord, as the one to whom you must give an account. Be ready to defend your faith — but do so with reverence and kindness, not with a defensiveness and haughtiness. In other words, 1 Peter is inviting us to act with integrity when we are being challenged, when we are uncomfortable. Former First Lady Michelle Obama once famously spoke about raising her daughters in the national spotlight, teaching them that "when they go low, we go high." That's the kind of thing that 1 Peter is commending here, in a Christian key.

Now, I do not know about you, but this kind of standard often feels to me as though it is way above my ability to fulfill. When someone questions, for example, my competence, or my sincerity, or my calling, my mind immediately goes down a very low road. "Don't fear what they fear," 1 Peter counsels, and truly I don't have to fear what *they* fear, because I have enough fears of my own. I fear looking silly before others. I fear appearing incompetent. I fear that someone will find my weaknesses and take advantage of them. In the face of such doubts, the larger truth about my life recedes into the background. I am loved and chosen by God, Jesus Christ is Lord and my detractors are not — when I become anxious, these convictions fade into the background of my consciousness. Maybe you, too, have a hard time showing reverence and kindness under pressure. Where are we supposed to get the grace to be the people God has made us to be? I know that I certainly do not have that strength within me — not on my own, anyway!

Where do we get that grace? 1 Peter suggests today that we look way outside of ourselves, to the victory that God is winning against sin and evil in all of creation. In other words, God gives us the grace by weaving our struggles, our suffering, into a wider cosmic picture.

In order to see this, we have to dig into the challenging parts of this passage. As I mentioned earlier, there are some complex aspects to this reading. I'm thinking in particular of verses 18 and 19, where the author tells us that Jesus "made proclamation to spirits in prison who in former times did not obey during the days of Noah." That is one of those passages that makes people think, "what is *this* about?" Is 1 Peter referring to spiritual beings who rebelled against God at that time? Or is this passage referring to the people, other than Noah, who were full of wickedness? Where is this prison, and how did Jesus make proclamation to the spirits there?

Now, if you find all of this confusing, please do not fault yourself: the Bible can be a very strange book. No one is completely certain what this passage means, even people who study the New Testament for a living! Here is what we do know: the story of the flood and Noah's ark is the story of a God who was deeply involved in dealing with human wickedness. The violence of the world at that time didn't just make God angry, it grieved God's heart. The flood was the expression of God's deep pain at the resistance of his creation. In saving Noah and his family, however, God continued to commit to all that God had made. The flood ends and life begins anew, and God promised that God will never again deal with evil by sending a flood. So how does God deal with evil? By sending Christ, as a sacrifice for sin, once and for all.

Now, there are so many questions to be asked about that and so many sermons that can be preached, but for our present purpose, I think this is what this means for us. God is involved with the battle of good over evil on the cosmic level. Jesus is at work in places that we know and in places that we do not know (think about that strange "prison" 1 Peter mentions!). God's work for good is as big as the flood. God's commitment to life is seen in every rainbow, a sign of the covenant made after the flood. When we feel that battle of good against evil come up in our own life situations, when we feel that battle rage in our minds, when we feel it rage on our lips, when it threatens our confidence that God has loved and chosen us, we can rest above all in this promise: God has sent Christ and in him has already proclaimed the victory. We are not the warriors. He is.

In Holy Baptism, we are joined to this victory that Christ has already won over evil. That is why 1 Peter can claim, with daring boldness, "Baptism now saves you, not as a removal of dirt from the body, but as the appeal of God for a good conscience." As God was with the flood, so in baptism God gets deeply involved with us, doing the work of bringing a new creation out in us. The Lutheran tradition in which I am ordained encourages baptized people to make remembrance of their baptism a daily reality. In our congregation, we have often celebrated Sunday school or confirmation lessons on baptism by having a swim party at a local pool or lake. We do this so that we can remind the kids that whenever they swim, or take a shower or a bath, or wash their face, or encounter water, they can remember that they are baptized. Baptism is a gift, a sacrament to rely on so that we do not have to rely on ourselves in the struggle that rages all around us.

I have discovered that this practice has come to mean something to our kids. They know, in ways that sometimes we adults don't like to admit, that it is hard to be the kind of people that God calls us to be. They know that it is hard, at times, to be kind, and that reverence isn't natural. They know that not all days are beautiful. God gives us something for those times: a promise, given with water, that we are loved and chosen.

Amen.

Ascension Day

Ephesians 1:15- 23

Power For Telling The Story

Happy Ascension Day, everyone! This is the one day on the church year in which Jesus seems to have some superhero qualities. He is lifted up, before the disciples, carried away on the clouds. He is, according to the script we say every week, "seated at the right hand of the father."

And, while the image of the superhero does not have lasting power when applied to Jesus, Ascension Day invites us to think about power — specifically, his resurrection power.

There is an icebreaker game, sometimes used also in job interviews, in which we ask the question, "if you had a superpower, what would it be and why?" The goal of the question, of course, is to help us think outside the limitations of human existence, to imagine what we would change, or what we could become, or where we could go, if we had no limits. The very presence of Jesus, risen from the dead, invites us to think outside the box in a very different way. If you had the power to overcome death, what would you do, and why? Or perhaps it would be better to say, "if you had access to someone who had overcome death, if you could draw on his power, what would you ask him to do and why?"

I want to think about that question, because one consequence of the Ascension is that we do have access to that power. Now that Jesus is seated at God's right hand, he is able to rule all things. He is no longer confined to space and time, but, as Ephesians tells us, is over all things, far above any other source of power. What's more, those who are part of his body, who relate to him in faith have access to his power, which is at work for those who believe. We have, in other words, access to the power of someone who has overcome death. So, how can we use it?

Now, the disciples who gathered with Jesus in the first forty days after his resurrection knew that when they were with him, they had access to that kind of amazing power. If you follow our first reading, from Acts, here is what they asked him, "Rabbi, is this the time when you will restore the kingdom to Israel?" It is a tragic question, because it betrays their pain and their hope. They knew that Jesus was king, risen from the dead. But they also knew that Pontius Pilate was still governor, that Herod was still a puppet king, and that Caesar still had his army. Jesus was risen, but any day could be someone else's Good Friday. Wouldn't it be amazing if Jesus could use his "superpower," his, I've-defeated-death-and-have-nothing-to-be-afraid of power, to get rid of the Romans and set the nation right? To fulfill ancient promises and make all things *good* again? What is Easter power for, if not to make all things good again, at least for them — for their, for their nation, for their tribe?

I don't know about you, but I can relate to that question. Lots of church folks do. For many of us, these times we are living in do not seem like "normal" times. Many of us wish we could get back to something. The 1950's, I am told, was a particularly good time for mainline churches; I've heard more than once the wish that things could be like that again. The 1990's seemed to be an optimistic time in the nation; I've heard, again more than once, that we could at least experience the calm of those days.

The ascension of Jesus tells us that Jesus is not in the business of using his I've-defeated-death-and-have-nothing-to-fear resurrection power to restore things to their former glory, at least not right now, and never for our small group. That is far too small a theater for all that God wants to do. Listen again to how Ephesians described Jesus' rule: he is above every rule, authority, power, dominion, and above every name that is named. He is above all those things not only in this age, but in all ages to come. He is Lord now as much as he was in the past and so will be for us in the future.

What will you use your superpower for, Jesus? We ask. He said to his disciples, "Wait for the spirit, and then I'm going to turn you into tellers of stories." You'll be my witnesses, he said. That word, witness, has two meanings. On the one hand, it means, people who have seen him, who know what he has done, healing people, breaking bread, forgiving sins. A witness is someone who knows who Jesus *was*. But in time — and all through the book of Acts — witnesses also meant people who could see what he is doing *now* — active as he is, all over the earth, not physically but in the power of the spirit. Witnesses are people who can remember and who can tell his story so completely that they are able to respond as it continues to unfold. Witnesses are people who, as Ephesians put it, "have the eyes of their hearts enlightened."

Ascension reveals that the promise of Easter is not that all things will become normal again or great again or stable again or whatever *we* imagine might be good. The promise is that we will be tellers of stories and bearers of hope. That *will* have an impact, even though Pontius Pilate is still governor, and Caesar still has armies, and people are very divided, and even though we sometimes feel awfully confused about how to be the church right now. Witness will have an impact, not because we have it figured out, but because Jesus promises to make it so.

The downtown community where the congregation I serve is located has a high poverty rate. Over the last thirty years, the downtown churches have cooperated to make sure that there is a free meal available every single day. The Lutherans have Monday and Thursday; the Methodists took Friday, the Presbyterians Wednesday, and so on. Whenever someone tells me the story of how those dinners began, someone often cites Jesus saying, "As often as you did it to the least of these, you have done it unto me." So then — *obviously* — when there were hungry people in Butler we had to feed them. That ongoing work of storytelling continues week in and week out, through good and bad seasons. Sometimes, we get really tired, and it seems as though energy and food is going to run out. Then someone, whose heart and eyes have been enlightened and who can see the immeasurable working of God's great power says something like, "Remember the feeding of the 5,000," and somehow the work continues.

It has become so much a part of who we are that it almost seems strange to think of it as Jesus' superpower, but this is what Jesus uses his Easter power for. To turn us into people who are able to talk about who he is. Into people who, knowing that he reigns in heaven, are also able to see his face in the face of a neighbor or a stranger, in the face of someone not at all like ourselves. He makes us into people who can see *his* hands and feet in the suffering of someone who is having their own Good Friday.

This is not a superpower the way we normally imagine it, but then again, Jesus' power never is. It is a power that is known in weakness: in the manger, on the cross. It is down to earth, yet it reigns on high. It is at work for us who believe.

Amen.

Seventh Sunday of Easter
1 Peter 4:12-14; 5:6-11

When The Way Of Life Is A Way Of Pain

Mr. Brock's second grade class was in an uproar. For a month, they had collecting small stuffed animals, pencils, erasers, and card games with the hope of putting together comfort kits for patients at the local children's hospital. However, the pile of stuffed animals meant for the kits had dwindled slowly and mysteriously over the last week. Mr. Brock was getting ready to confront the school security staff when five of the missing stuffies were found hidden in Jeremy's cubby.

Parents were called and consequences were assessed. Jeremy returned the stuffed animals to the pile and apologized to the class. Mr. Brock had hoped that Jeremy would learn a lesson, that the project could go forward. But second graders have their own form of social punishment, and later that day, Jeremy had no one to sit with at lunch. On the playground, people refused to play with him. "Thief!" one of them yelled. "You *stole*!"

Another little boy, Tyrell, watched with unease. He came from a family that talked about forgiveness and from a church where "confession and assurance of pardon" happened every week in the Sunday liturgy. He regularly prayed the Lord's prayer to "forgive us our sins and we forgive those who trespass against us." Tyrell went to Jeremy and told him that he forgave him and that they could still be friends.

Now, in an ideal world, this would have been the beginning of a sweet story. This would be the moment when Tyrell's offer of forgiveness and friendship would lead to reconciliation between Jeremy and the whole class. Jeremy would never steal again and so reformed, he would be embraced by his classmates and even make new friends. Everyone would remember that learning hard lessons is part of being a kid, and life would go on as planned.

It didn't happen that way for Jeremy and Tyrell. What happened was that the next day, Tyrell sat with Jeremy, and the rest of the class started to call *him* a thief, too. "You're no better than a thief if you're a thief's friend," they cried.

Tyrell went home despondent. He asked his dad (from whom I heard this story): I thought that I was doing everything that God wanted me to do! Why is everyone being so mean to me?

I thought that I was doing what God wanted me to do, so why are they hurting me? Tyrell discovered one of the most difficult truths, and one of the deepest paradoxes, of the Christian faith. Following Jesus is the way to life, but that way to life often includes a lot of pain and rejection.

This Easter season, we have celebrated God's greatest gifts: new life, new creation, reconciliation, grace itself. These are the values of God's kingdom. When they are put into practice and claimed as a way of life in the world, these values are profoundly countercultural. In a world where the precious things of life are bought and sold as commodities, it is countercultural that Christians will often give food away to the hungry as part of their ministry. In a world that says, "we like people who look like us and who talk like us," it is countercultural that Christians welcome immigrants and refugees. In a world that says, "what goes around comes around," it is countercultural that Christians forgive. I've seen Christians do all of these things at the risk of being different than the prevailing values in their neighborhood. Difference can be uncomfortable and cause significant conflict and sometimes we take the heat.

1 Peter called this phenomenon "suffering as a Christian," and suggested that we not be surprised when it happens. "Don't be surprised at the fiery ordeal that's taking place among you," the scripture reads. We don't know exactly what

that ordeal was for that little church. We *do* know what it has looked like in other places. In 295, Maximilian of Tebessa refused to be fitted for Roman armor and accept the emperor' seal, claiming that as a Christian he could not join the military. He was the first conscientious objector to war in the Christian tradition, a conviction he paid for with his life.

The Christian tradition discourages seeking out such martyrdom. Scripture is clear, however, that faithful living may result in rejection by your own people, neighbors, family, or the people with whom you share a classroom, a workplace, or an address. "Pick up your cross and follow me," was the way that Jesus put it. The sinner side of us will reject that this has to be, will wonder whether something has gone wrong, will question the power or the motives of a God who seems to will such rejection upon those God loves. The sinful side of us wants to believe that faith in God should somehow be easier than it is.

If the way of love were easy, it would not have resulted in a cross. But the cross is what love looks like in this world. The good news is that we are joined to Christ. And because we have been joined to Christ, the suffering we experience on the path of discipleship is not our own, it is his. He bears it with us and for us. In exchange, he gives us the victory of his risen life.

Jesus doesn't promise ease, but he does promise support. He is there with us to share the burden. For he is alive and continues his work. For he is risen! Risen indeed.

Amen.

In Every Language Under Heaven

Some time ago, I was standing in line to use the ATM at our local bank. At this bank, as in many places, the first question that the ATM will ask when you insert your card is to choose a language. In our case, you get a choice of about eight: English, Spanish, Portuguese, German, Chinese, Korean, and so forth. On this day, the woman in front of me seemed annoyed by the question. "I just don't understand why we have to have all these languages on these things. Why can't we all speak English?"

It's hard for me to retell it in quite the way that she said it, but she was really mad, and I don't think that it was just because she had to spend two seconds of time to hit the English button and get on with it. Language is more than a way of saying "hello" or "goodbye." Languages are powerful unifiers, but they also mark out our differences. They are part of group identity, who is in and who is out. When politicians in our country speak about having English be the national language, they tap into our desire for unity and our discomfort with difference. When Europeans conquered the lands of the Africa and the new world, they often outlawed the use of native languages as a way of consolidating power and communicating who was in charge. My great-grandmother was the child of German immigrants, and her family went to a Lutheran congregation that spoke German — until what was then known as the Great War began, and suddenly, to prove their loyalty, German Lutherans started using English instead. Teenagers in school differentiate themselves from their parents by creating new slang. Just think: what was the *cat's meow* of the 1940s became *groovy* in the '60s became rad in the '80s and *phat* around the year 2000, leading parents of *every* generation to say, "Can't we just all speak normally?"

Given how central languages are to our identity, the story of Pentecost seems as much a challenge for our thinking as it does a miracle to amaze us. Before Peter preached or before Stephen was stoned, before the scales fell from Paul's eyes and well before the church as we know it came to be, the Holy Spirit's first miracle was *translation*. The Holy Spirit came down with a rush of wind and tongues of fire and caused the disciples to speak every language known on earth. I've been a part of some congregations that celebrate this festival by having the lessons read in in languages other than English. In this way, we remember that the church does not just speak English.

I wonder what it must have been like to be there, that first Pentecost, to witness that translation for the first time. Acts tells us that there were a lot of immigrants living in Jerusalem at that time. "Devout Jews," the text tells us, from every nation under heaven, living in Jerusalem. Did you catch that long list in the story? Parthians, Medes, Elamites, residents of Mesopotamia, Judea, and Cappodocia, Pontus and Asia, Phrygia and Pamphylia, Egypt and parts of Libya belonging to Cyrene, visitors from Rome, Cretans and Arabs, people who did not share the native language of their neighbors, people all who probably felt always a little different, with their funny accents and their imperfect speech. No wonder when the Spirit rained fire from heaven they were drawn to the house. "What is this about?" they wondered. "What does this mean? In our own native language, we hear them speaking about God's deeds of power." At the moment when people heard the gospel in their own native language, they also saw others, who were different than they were, hearing the gospel in *their* own native languages. That is the grace of Pentecost. God deeply desires to speak to us through our native, heart language and also that God wants us to recognize that "our own" language isn't enough. God has opened the door to our hearts and leads us to see that the door is opened wide for others, too.

It's usually easy enough to believe that God speaks to us through our own native languages. My husband, who grew up in the Netherlands, always teases me that I have to work on my mastery of Dutch — *his* native language — because he claims that it is the language of heaven. If I want to be able to sing when I get there, I'd better start practicing now. For almost all of us, our first language is the language of our hearts, and for many of us, it is the language of worship. It's why the Bible translation that we grew up with is usually our favorite and why it's hard to adjust to a new version of the Lord's Prayer or the Apostles' Creed. God uses words to reach us. Familiar words. Words spoken in the mouths of trusted parents or grandparents or Sunday school teachers or friends that communicated that God loved you. So, it's easy to believe that the Holy Spirit uses our native languages, our heart languages, to speak to us about God's deeds of power.

It's harder, however, to believe to trust that the good news comes also through languages *other* than our own native language. If the world had designed Pentecost, we would have designed a completely different miracle. We probably would have told the Holy Spirit to come down and make us all the same, speaking the *same* language. It would have been so much easier!

Why can't we just all speak English? Why can't we just all speak one language around here? Truth is, it would be easier if we could. But God refuses to be boiled down to that which is easy and comfortable to us. Pentecost summons us to faith in God who is bigger than what we can imagine. The Holy Spirit is at worked can use those languages that just seem so strange to us, to speak of the mighty deeds of God and call our neighbors into faith. There are many languages, many Bible translations, many forms of music...and yet, there is one Lord, one faith, one baptism, one God and Father of all, and we were baptized into one Spirit. Whether we worship in America or Tanzania or the Netherlands or Puerto Rico, God sees the church, as the single body of his son. The miracle of Pentecost happens every baptism, when in faith each baptized person is joined to Christ and to the body of Christ throughout the world. Whether that baptism happens in the name of the Father and of the Son and of the Holy Spirit, or in *el nombre del Padre y del Hijo y del Espiritu Santo* or in *de naam van de Vadder en van de Zoon en van de Heilige Geest*…it is all baptism in one triune name.

Why does the Holy Spirit bother? I can only imagine that it is because that when it comes to the kingdom of God, there is no "right," language. There is only the gracious decision of God to reach us in Jesus Christ. You can't earn a place by speaking the right language. Our diversity — within the congregation, and within the whole church, is simply a sign of God's desire to reach us. We need our own language in order to hear the gospel; we need others with their other languages to remind us of just how wide and deep and rich the gospel really is.

There's news in that, for this world, which grows more global by the day and in which we are constantly more and more languages to choose from at the ATM. The power of the Spirit can transform the differences and the diversity that cause us such discomfort. In the power of the Spirit, that person who comes into your office and seems only to speak Spanish may just be someone that God will use to talk to you. In baptism of the Spirit, we're connected.

Friends, I do not know where or how you will experience the great diversity of language that God has given us, but I pray that when you do, you will think on the story of Acts and the Spirit's baptism, and you will receive your neighbors as a gift.

Amen.

www.ingramcontent.com/pod-product-compliance
Lightning Source LLC
LaVergne TN
LVHW091207080426
835509LV00006B/877